About Mollusks

About Mollusks

A Guide for Children

Cathryn Sill

Illustrated by John Sill

Ω
PEACHTREE
ATLANTA

For the One who created mollusks.

—*Genesis* 1:25

Published by
PEACHTREE PUBLISHERS
1700 Chattahoochee Avenue
Atlanta, Georgia 30318-2112
www.peachtree-online.com

ISBN 1-56145-331-5

Illustrations created in watercolor on archival quality 100% rag watercolor paper

Printed in Singapore
10 9 8 7 6 5 4 3 2 1
First Edition

Library of Congress Cataloging-in-Publication Data

Sill, Cathryn P., 1953-
   About mollusks / written by Cathryn Sill ; illustrated by John Sill.-- 1st ed.
      p. cm.
   Includes bibliographical references and index.
   ISBN 1-56145-331-5 (alk. paper)
   1. Mollusks--Juvenile literature. I. Sill, John, ill. II. Title.

QL405.2.S56 2005
594--dc22
                        2004017719

About Mollusks

Mollusks have soft, moist bodies
with no bones.

Most mollusks have hard shells that protect their soft bodies.

Mollusk shells grow from a special organ called a mantle. The mantle is a skinlike fold that covers their bodies.

Some mollusks do not have a shell.

Baby mollusks grow from eggs.

Most mollusks live in water.

Those that live on land make slime to help them move along.

The slime also keeps their bodies from drying out.

PLATE 8
Florida Tree Snails

Most mollusks have a muscle called a "foot" that helps them travel from place to place.

Some mollusks use their foot to burrow in sand or mud.

Some mollusks move by sucking water into their body and squirting it out quickly.

Other kinds of mollusks attach themselves
to one place and stay there.

Many mollusks are predators—they hunt
and eat other animals.

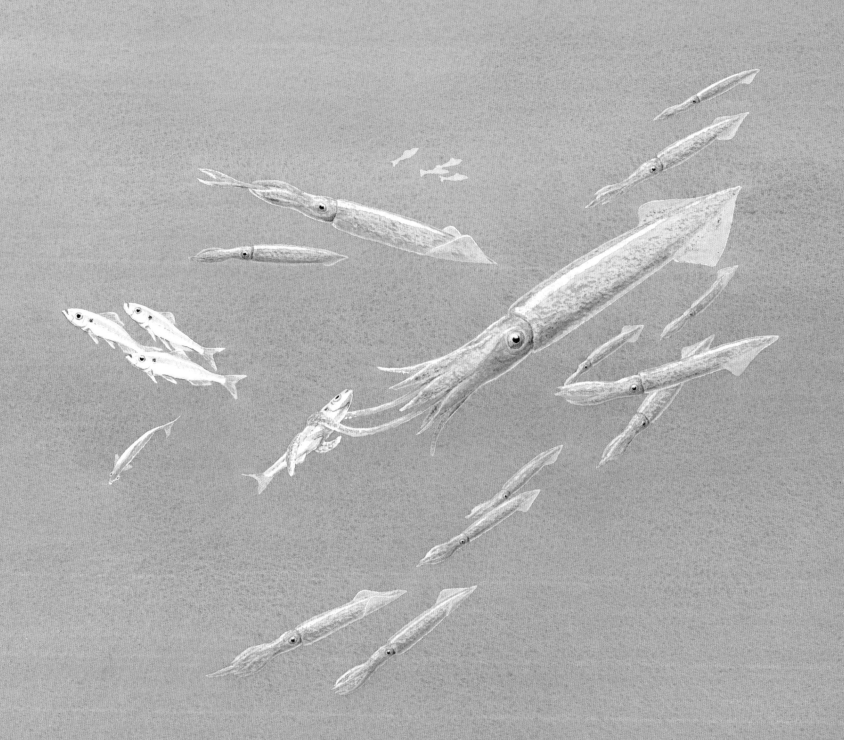

Mollusks with two-part shells filter food out of the water around them.

PLATE 14
Soft-shelled Clam

Some mollusks have a rough tongue that can scrape off bits of plants to eat.

Mollusks provide food for many animals and people.

Mollusks are a valuable part of our world. It is important to protect them and the places where they live.

Afterword

PLATE 1

Mollusks are a phylum—a large division of the animal kingdom—of different animals, including gastropods (snails and slugs), bivalves (clams, oysters, and scallops), and cephalopods (squids and octopuses). There are over 50,000 species of mollusks, ranging from tiny sea snails to very large squids and octopuses. Giant Pacific Octopuses (16 feet long and weighing 50–90 pounds*) live along the Pacific Coast of North America, near rocky shores and in tide pools. Octopuses have larger and more complex brains than other animals without backbones. Experiments have shown that they are able to learn tasks like solving mazes and removing the lids from jars.

PLATE 2

Shells protect the bodies of mollusks in various ways. Some shells are camouflaged to look like their surroundings, making them hard for predators to detect. The slippery shells of some mollusks allow them to slide out of their enemies' grasp. The knobs and spines on the shell of the Horse Conch make the animal seem larger to its predators, or harder to swallow. Horse Conchs (18–24 inches long) are the largest snails in North America. They live on sandy bottoms in shallow water below the low-tide line on the coast from North Carolina to Texas.

PLATE 3

Mollusk shells may have one part (snails), two parts (clams, oysters), or eight parts (chitons). Mantles cause the shells to grow as the animals grow. Long after the animals die, the shells remain. When Flamingo Tongues (1 inch long) push out their brightly colored mantles, the mantles can completely cover their white shells. These animals live on Sea Fans and Sea Whips and eat the tiny coral polyps. Flamingo Tongues are found in shallow ocean water along the Atlantic Coast from North Carolina to the Bahamas.

* Sizes vary. All measurements in the Afterword are approximate, and are for adult animals.

PLATE 4

Mantles protect the bodies of mollusks that do not have shells. Sea slugs, or nudibranchs, have shells when they first hatch, but the shells disappear as they mature into adults. Many sea slugs have bright colors and strange shapes. Hopkins' Roses (1 inch long) are bright pink nudibranchs that eat a pink species of bryozoan (tiny aquatic animals) and lay a pink mass of eggs. They live near the low-tide line along the Pacific Coast of North America.

PLATE 5

Some mollusks lay eggs that float in water. Others fasten their eggs to seaweed or rocks. Some lay eggs in ribbons of jelly. Others lay their eggs in clusters. Some snail eggs grow inside the mother's body. Whelks lay eggs in protective cases. Their empty egg-case strings often wash up on beaches. Lightning Whelks (6–10 inches long) live on sandy bottoms along the coast from North Carolina to Texas. They are one of the few snails that have the opening on the left side of the shell.

PLATE 6

The largest numbers of mollusks live in oceans. Some live in freshwater streams, ponds, and lakes. Common Violet Snails (1 1/2 inches long) blow bubbles that harden and make a raft. They cling to the underside of the bubbles and float around on the ocean surface searching for food. Common Violet Snails are found worldwide in tropical and subtropical waters.

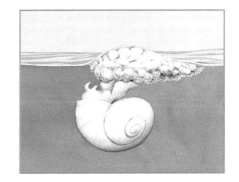

PLATE 7

Land mollusks usually live in damp places. Their skin makes mucus that leaves a slimy track as they crawl slowly from place to place. Banana Slugs (8 inches long) can move at a speed of about 25 feet per hour. A native of the moist forest floors of the northern Pacific Coast, Banana Slugs are the largest land mollusk in North America.

PLATE 8

Land mollusks will die if their damp bodies dry out. During the dry season, Florida Tree Snails (2 inches long) attach to tree trunks and seal themselves off with mucus to preserve their body moisture. This period of inactivity is called estivation. Florida Tree Snails are becoming scarcer because of shell collectors and loss of habitat.

PLATE 9

Many mollusks use their foot for crawling. Some bivalves wedge their foot between rocks and pull their body along. Some mollusks may also use their foot to pry open clams or oysters to eat. Purple-ringed Top Shells (1 1/2 inches long, 1 1/4 inches wide) are fast for snails. In one experiment, some of these snails moved 30 feet in 24 hours when they were released at the base of kelp plants. Purple-ringed Top Shells are natives of the Pacific Coast of North America.

PLATE 10

Variable Coquinas (3/4 inch long) follow the tides. When a wave tosses them on to the beach, they burrow into the sand just below the surface, where they filter food from the water. These colorful little mollusks, often found on the beaches of the southeastern United States, are sometimes called "butterfly shells."

PLATE 11

Pacific Pink Scallops (2 1/2 inches wide) "swim" away from danger by opening their shells to suck in water. Then they clap their shells together, squirting the water out their sides in jets that propel them forward. The shells often do not look pink because they are covered with sponges. The sponges provide camouflage for the scallops, and the scallops provide the sponges a way to escape from predators. Pacific Pink Scallops live in the eastern Pacific Ocean.

PLATE 12

Oyster larvae (newly hatched oysters) only move around until they find a place to stay. The oyster rubs its foot over the area it has chosen and makes cement that sticks its shell to that place. From then on, its only movement is opening and closing its shell to get food. Eastern Oysters (3–8 inches long) have been an important source of food for people since prehistoric times. Today, many of the large oyster beds along the Atlantic Coast are in danger because of pollution.

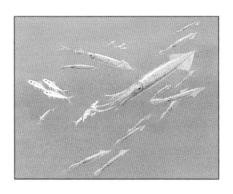

PLATE 13

Cephalopods hunt by grabbing prey with their arms and biting it with their strong beaklike mouths. Squid usually travel in groups. They capture prey with their tentacles. Northern Shortfin Squid (12 inches long) move in fast, aggressive packs that attack schools of small fish. These mollusks live along the Atlantic Coast from North Carolina to Newfoundland.

PLATE 14

Bivalves get food by sucking water between their shells and straining tiny plants and animals from it. The water is drawn in either through the open edge of the shells or through tubes called siphons. Soft-shelled Clams (3–6 inches long) may burrow more than 10 inches deep in sand or mud with their siphons extended near the surface. A spurt of water squirts out of the hole in the mud when the clam pulls its siphon back into its shell. These clams are found on both coasts of North America.

PLATE 15

Many mollusks have a radula, a sort of tongue with rows of tiny teeth. They use their tongues to scrape off bits of plants or meat to eat. Meat eaters have tongues with fewer teeth that are sharp and strong. Plant eaters have broad radulas with thousands of teeth. Garden Snails (1 1/2 inches wide) were introduced to North America from Europe. They are serious pests in many gardens because they eat leafy plants.

PLATE 16

Mollusks are an important part of the food chain. Because they are so abundant, they provide food for organisms in many different habitats. Humans harvest clams, oysters, snails, and other mollusks for food. Many animals feed on mollusks. Florida Apple Snails (2 1/2 inches long), found in freshwater swamps, ponds, and rivers, are the main food for Snail Kites. The long curved bill of the Snail Kite is perfectly designed to pull the mollusk meat from the shell.

PLATE 17

Mollusks serve many useful purposes. Since ancient times, people have used the shells of mollusks for a wide variety of products, including money, jewelry, buttons, and calcium supplements. Today, mollusks are an important part of the fishing industry. Some mollusks help preserve water quality by filtering dangerous toxins from the water. The popularity of shell collecting has reduced the numbers of mollusks in many areas. Lined Chitons' (1 1/2 inches long) shells are made up of eight valves, or parts, fitted together like a plate of armor. They are not easy to see because their colors so closely match the algae they feed on, but the sight of one is worth the search. Lined Chitons live in intertidal rocky areas along the Pacific Coast of North America.

BIBLIOGRAPHY

BOOKS

Berrill, N.J., and Jacquelyn Berrill. *1001 Questions Answered About the Seashore*. New York: Dover Publications, Inc., 1957.

Burnie, David. *The Kingfisher Illustrated Animal Encyclopedia*. New York: Kingfisher, 2000.

Cassie, Brian. *National Audubon Society First Field Guide: Shells*. New York: Scholastic, Inc., 2000.

Meinkoth, Norman A. *National Audubon Society Field Guide to North American Seashore Creatures*. New York: Alfred A Knopf, 1998.

Richardson, Joy. *Mollusks*. New York: Franklin Watts, 1993.

Stone, Lynn. *Slugs and Snails (Creepy Crawlers Discovery Library)*. Vero Beach, FL: The Rourke Book Co., Inc., 1995.

WEBSITES

www.eNature.com
www.nps.gov
www.oceanicresearch.org
www.cephbase.utmb.edu
www.seaotter.com
www.seaslugforum.net

Also in the ABOUT… series

Cathryn Sill, a former elementary school teacher, is the author of the acclaimed ABOUT… series. With her husband John and her brother-in-law Ben Sill, she coauthored the popular bird-guide parodies, A FIELD GUIDE TO LITTLE-KNOWN AND SELDOM-SEEN BIRDS OF NORTH AMERICA, ANOTHER FIELD GUIDE TO LITTLE-KNOWN AND SELDOM-SEEN BIRDS OF NORTH AMERICA, and BEYOND BIRDWATCHING, all from Peachtree Publishers.

John Sill is a prize-winning and widely published wildlife artist who illustrated the ABOUT… series and coauthored the FIELD GUIDES and BEYOND BIRDWATCHING. A native of North Carolina, he holds a B.S. in Wildlife Biology from North Carolina State University.

The Sills live and work in Franklin, North Carolina.